P9-ARO-757

Tools

Search

Notes

Discuss

MyReportLinks.com Books

Go!

PRESIDENTS

JAMES MONROE

A MyReportLinks.com Book

Tim O'Shei & Joe Marren

 MyReportLinks.com Books
an imprint of
Enslow Publishers, Inc.
Box 398, 40 Industrial Road
Berkeley Heights, NJ 07922
USA

MyReportLinks.com Books, an imprint of Enslow Publishers, Inc.

Library of Congress Cataloging-in-Publication Data

O'Shei, Tim.
     James Monroe / Tim O'Shei & Joe Marren.
       p. cm. — (Presidents)
      Summary: Examines the life of the president known for the foreign
policy which bears his name, the Monroe Doctrine. Includes Internet
links to Web sites, source documents,
and photographs related to Monroe's life.
     Includes bibliographical references and index.
     ISBN 0-7660-5076-9
     1. Monroe, James, 1758–1831—Juvenile literature. 2. Presidents—United
States—Biography—Juvenile literature. [1. Monroe, James, 1758–1831.
2. Presidents.] I. Marren, Joe. II. Title. III. Series.
E372.O84 2002
973.5'4'092—dc21
[B]
                            2001008210

Printed in the United States of America

10 9 8 7 6 5 4 3 2 1

To Our Readers:
Through the purchase of this book, you and your library gain access to the Report Links that specifically back up this book.
The Publisher will provide access to the Report Links that back up this book and will keep these Report Links up to date on **www.myreportlinks.com** for three years from the book's first publication date.
We have done our best to make sure all Internet addresses in this book were active and appropriate when we went to press. However, the author and the Publisher have no control over, and assume no liability for, the material available on those Internet sites or on other Web sites they may link to.
The usage of the MyReportLinks.com Books Web site is subject to the terms and conditions stated on the Usage Policy Statement on **www.myreportlinks.com**.
In the future, a password may be required to access the Report Links that back up this book. The password is found on the bottom of page 4 of this book.
Any comments or suggestions can be sent by e-mail to comments@myreportlinks.com or to the address on the back cover.

Photo Credits: © Corel Corporation, pp. 1 (background), 3; Courtesy of America's Story from America's Library/Library of Congress, pp. 13, 14; Courtesy of American Memory/Library of Congress, p. 24; Courtesy of Monticello Avenue, pp. 22, 25, 34, 44; Courtesy of MyReportLinks.com Books, p. 4; Courtesy of Swem Library, College of William and Mary, p. 18; Courtesy of The American Presidency/Smithsonian Institution, p. 17; Courtesy of The American President/PBS, p. 42; Courtesy of The White House Historical Association, p. 21; Department of the Interior, p. 31, 36; Dover Publications, Inc., © 1967, pp. 28 (Elizabeth Monroe), 39; Library of Congress, pp. 1, 26, 29, 30; Painting by Charles Wilson Peale (Lafayette), p. 28; Painting by John Trumbull, p. 19; U.S. Capitol Collection, p. 38.

Cover Photo: © Corel Corporation; James Monroe by Rembrant Peale, donated by Camilla Hoes Pope in memory of her husband Laurence Gouverneur Hoes. Courtesy of the James Monroe Museum and Memorial Library, Fredericksburg, Virginia.

Tools

Search

Notes
Discuss

MyReportLinks.com Books

Go!

Contents

MyReportLinks.com Books
Great Books, Great Links, Great for Research!

MyReportLinks.com Books present the information you need to learn about your report subject. In addition, they show you where to go on the Internet for more information. The pre-evaluated Report Links that back up this book are kept up to date on **www.myreportlinks.com**. With the purchase of a MyReportLinks.com Books title, you and your library gain access to the Report Links that specifically back up that book. The Report Links save hours of research time and link to dozens—even hundreds—of Web sites, source documents, and photos related to your report topic.

Please see "To Our Readers" on the Copyright page for important information about this book, the MyReportLinks.com Books Web site, and the Report Links that back up this book.

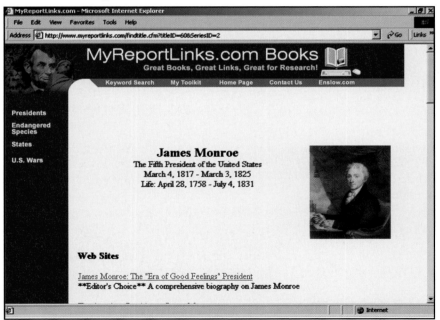

Access:

The Publisher will provide access to the Report Links that back up this book and will try to keep these Report Links up to date on our Web site for three years from the book's first publication date. Please enter **PMO1513** if asked for a password.

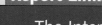

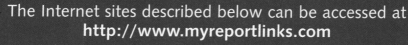
The Internet sites described below can be accessed at
http://www.myreportlinks.com

*EDITOR'S CHOICE

▶**James Monroe: The "Era of Good Feelings" President**
Here you will learn about James Monroe's life before, during, and
after his presidency. You will also find information about Monroe's
family, as well as the impact of his time in office.

Link to this Internet site from http://www.myreportlinks.com

*EDITOR'S CHOICE

▶**The American Presidency: James Monroe**
This comprehensive biography of James Monroe includes information
about his early career, opposition to the Federalists, role as a diplomat for
Jefferson, Cabinet membership, presidency, the acquisition of Florida, the
Monroe Doctrine, domestic controversies, and his retirement.

Link to this Internet site from http://www.myreportlinks.com

*EDITOR'S CHOICE

▶**The American President: "The World Stage"**
At this PBS Web site, four presidents are featured who were thought to
have succeeded at representing the nation at a critical time, including
James Monroe. Here you will find a brief essay about Monroe, a video
clip, and a historical document.

Link to this Internet site from http://www.myreportlinks.com

*EDITOR'S CHOICE

▶**Objects from the Presidency**
By navigating through this site you will find objects related to all the
United States presidents, including James Monroe. You can also read
a brief description of the era he lived in and learn about the office of
the presidency.

Link to this Internet site from http://www.myreportlinks.com

*EDITOR'S CHOICE

▶**James Monroe Sought Advice from Thomas Jefferson**
America's Story from America's Library, a Library of Congress Web site,
provides this feature about James Monroe's decision on whether to take the
advice of Thomas Jefferson and James Madison or of John Quincy Adams
when he issued the Monroe Doctrine.

Link to this Internet site from http://www.myreportlinks.com

*EDITOR'S CHOICE

▶**"I Do Solemnly Swear . . ."**
At this Web site you will find James Monroe's 1817 inaugural address,
facts about the address, and portraits of the president.

Link to this Internet site from http://www.myreportlinks.com

The Internet sites described below can be accessed at
http://www.myreportlinks.com

▶**American Presidents: Life Portraits**
This brief outline of facts about President Monroe includes information about his children, religion, military service, and assorted public service information. You will also find a letter written by James Monroe.

Link to this Internet site from http://www.myreportlinks.com

▶**The American Presidency: Daniel D. Tompkins**
At this Web site you will find a brief biography of Daniel D. Tompkins, James Monroe's vice president. Here you learn about his political career and vice presidency.

Link to this Internet site from http://www.myreportlinks.com

▶**The American Revolution: James Monroe**
This James Monroe biography includes in-depth discussions of his early career, his anti-Federalist beliefs, his work as a diplomat for Jefferson, and his time spent as a Cabinet member and president.

Link to this Internet site from http://www.myreportlinks.com

▶**Ash Lawn – Highland**
At this Web site you will find a brief biography about James Monroe, tour information, and a map of the area. You can also take a virtual tour of Ash Lawn.

Link to this Internet site from http://www.myreportlinks.com

▶**The Avalon Project: The Papers of James Monroe**
The Yale Law School Avalon Project Web site contains links to Monroe's inaugural addresses, the Monroe Doctrine, and his correspondence with Charles Baggot on the Exchange of Notes Relative to Naval Forces.

Link to this Internet site from http://www.myreportlinks.com

▶**Echoes from the White House**
By navigating through the different time periods, you will learn about important events that took place in the White House. You can also take a virtual tour.

Link to this Internet site from http://www.myreportlinks.com

Report Links

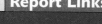

The Internet sites described below can be accessed at
http://www.myreportlinks.com

▶**James Madison and James Monroe**

At this Web site you will find an essay that explores the lives of
James Monroe and James Madison. Here you will learn how the
lives of Monroe and Madison were similar in many ways.

Link to this Internet site from http://www.myreportlinks.com

▶**James Monroe**

This Web site includes a brief biography of James Monroe that focuses
on his role as a soldier in the Revolutionary War. You will also find a
general list of facts about his life.

Link to this Internet site from http://www.myreportlinks.com

▶**James Monroe**

At this Web site you will find an outline of information about James
Monroe including election results, Cabinet members, notable events,
points of interest, and useful links.

Link to this Internet site from http://www.myreportlinks.com

▶**James Monroe**

At this Web site you will find a general biography about President
Monroe, which focuses primarily on his political views, his role
in important events in United States history, and highlights of
his presidency.

Link to this Internet site from http://www.myreportlinks.com

▶**James Monroe**

At the National Gallery of Art Web site, you will find Gilbert Stuart's
portrait of James Monroe and details about the painting.

Link to this Internet site from http://www.myreportlinks.com

▶**James Monroe – Biography**

This James Monroe biography gives an in-depth explanation of the
Missouri Compromise and the Monroe Doctrine, as well as links to his
election results and inaugural addresses.

Link to this Internet site from http://www.myreportlinks.com

The Internet sites described below can be accessed at
http://www.myreportlinks.com

▶**James Monroe: Fifth United States President**
The Manuscripts and Rare Books Department at Swem Library of the College
of William and Mary, offers images from its collection of original portraits and
rare documents related to James Monroe. You will also find brief biography
and other helpful links.

Link to this Internet site from http://www.myreportlinks.com

▶**James Monroe's Home Page**
This site includes a James Monroe history page, a pictures page, a links page,
and a Quick Facts page.

Link to this Internet site from http://www.myreportlinks.com

▶**James Monroe Museum and Memorial Library**
At this Web site you will find list of information about the James Monroe
Museum including general information, highlights, exhibits, events, and
photographs of James Monroe paraphernalia.

Link to this Internet site from http://www.myreportlinks.com

▶**James Monroe, Views of the President of the United States
on the Subject of Internal Improvements**
This 1822 essay by President Monroe is focused primarily on his opinions
regarding the roles of national and local governments in internal
improvements, taxes, and duties.

Link to this Internet site from http://www.myreportlinks.com

▶**James Monroe (1758–1831)**
Here you will find a list of links to James Monroe's First and Second
Inaugural Addresses, his eight State of the Nation Addresses, and the
Monroe Doctrine.

Link to this Internet site from http://www.myreportlinks.com

▶**James Monroe (1758–1831)**
At the National Portrait Gallery you will find an oil painting of James
Monroe. You can also read a brief description of Monroe's presidency.

Link to this Internet site from http://www.myreportlinks.com

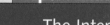
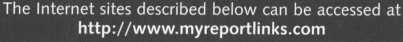

The Internet sites described below can be accessed at
http://www.myreportlinks.com

▶**Missouri Compromise**
At this PBS Web site you will find a brief explanation of the Missouri
Compromise, as well as the complete text of the historic document.

Link to this Internet site from http://www.myreportlinks.com

▶**Today in History**
At this Web site you can read a letter written by James Monroe to
Thomas Jefferson regarding foreign policy. You will also learn how
Theodore Roosevelt added the "Roosevelt Corollary" to the Monroe
Doctrine in 1904.

Link to this Internet site from http://www.myreportlinks.com

▶**White House Historical Association**
At the White House Historical Association you can explore the rich
history of the White House and the presidents of the United States.
You can also take a virtual tour of the White House, visit the
president's park, and experience past presidential inaugurations.

Link to this Internet site from http://www.myreportlinks.com

▶**White House: Elizabeth Kortright Monroe**
The official White House Web site holds the biography of Elizabeth
Kortright Monroe. Here you will learn about her life and experiences
in the White House.

Link to this Internet site from http://www.myreportlinks.com

▶**White House: James Monroe**
The official White House biography of James Monroe provides a brief
overview of his presidency and general facts about his accomplishments.

Link to this Internet site from http://www.myreportlinks.com

▶**What a Difference One Vote Makes**
This PBS site provides a brief overview of the Election of 1820 and the
electoral college. Here you will learn how one vote almost cost James
Monroe the election.

Link to this Internet site from http://www.myreportlinks.com

Highlights

1758—*April 28:* Born in Westmoreland County, Virginia.

1774—Father, Spence, dies when James is sixteen. Enters the College of William & Mary in Virginia.

1776—*March:* Monroe joins the Continental Army and rises from lieutenant to major.

1780–1783—Studies law under Thomas Jefferson in Virginia.

1782–1783—Serves in the Virginia Assembly.

1783–1786—Serves three one-year terms in the Continental Congress.

1786—*Feb. 16:* Marries Elizabeth Kortright in New York City.

1787—Daughter, Eliza, is born.

1789—Loses election to Congress to James Madison by three hundred votes.

1790–1794—Serves as U.S. senator.

1794–1796—Minister to France; recalled by President Washington.

1799–1802—Serves as Governor of Virginia.

1803—Daughter, Maria Hester, is born.

1803–1807—Minister to England.

1810–1811—Serves in the Virginia assembly.

1811—*Jan.–March:* Again serves as Governor of Virginia.

1811–1817—Serves as Secretary of State.

1814–1815—Serves as Secretary of War.

1816—Defeats Rufus King to become the fifth president.

1817—*March 4:* Inaugurated president. Daniel D. Tompkins is his vice president.

1819—Spain cedes Florida to the United States.

—Panic of 1819 economic depression.

1820—Missouri Compromise allows admission of Missouri as a slave state and Maine as a free state.

1821—*March 5:* Inaugurated for his second term as president.

1823—*Dec. 2:* Delivers Monroe Doctrine.

1830—*Sept. 23:* Wife, Elizabeth Monroe dies.

1831—*July 4:* Monroe dies in New York City.

1858—Body reburied in Richmond, Virginia.

Chapter 1

Tough Words on the Home Turf, 1823

James Monroe had an important decision to make. That much he knew. Still, the president could not have forseen that his choice would affect people for centuries.

The year was 1823. The world was changing. Mexico, the United States' southern neighbor, broke free of Spanish rule in 1821. That meant the United States had a new, independent neighbor to the south. But that was not all: Three South American lands—Argentina, Chile, and Columbia—had also been fighting for their freedom from Spain. In 1822, they had won their independence as well.

▶ Staking Out the Globe

So now four new independent countries were forming in the Western Hemisphere. Why would this be a problem? After all, the United States had been founded on the concept of freedom. Spain, of course, was unhappy. No country likes to lose its colonies, especially in a fight. Spain wanted its colonies back, and it was likely that four other European governments (France, Austria, Prussia, and Russia) were going to help seize those lands.

For Monroe, that was the problem. As president of the United States, it was his job to ensure that American land was safe from invasion from foreign countries. The possibility of a European alliance fighting the Mexicans and many South Americans, trying to take back the land, was unsettling. For Americans, that kind of war was too close to home. Monroe had to protect his own land, and it

was always a good idea to help his neighbors, too. So now, Monroe felt he had to do something.

He was not alone. Great Britain was also concerned. After the new countries broke free of Spain, the British had started a profitable trade with them. Not wanting to lose that source of money and goods, Great Britain asked the United States if it would join it in making a declaration. They wished to state that all of North, Central, and South America was off-limits. Basically, Britain wanted the United States to join it in stating that other countries could not develop colonies in the entire Western Hemisphere.

Many people in the United States sympathized with the people in the former Spanish colonies. It had only been forty-seven years since the United States had broken away from Great Britain and fought a war for its freedom. Many of those freedom fighters were still alive. Monroe himself had fought in the Revolutionary War. So there was a sense in America that it would be good to help another group of former colonies keep their independence.

▶ Shutting Out the British

Not all Americans liked the idea of accepting help from the British. Only a decade earlier, the United States had fought Britain a second time during the War of 1812. Plenty of Americans still had bad feelings toward Britain. Not sure what to do, President Monroe talked to two people he trusted deeply: Thomas Jefferson and James Madison. Both former presidents—and both friends of Monroe— Jefferson and Madison told him that it would be good to make the statement with British backing. Next, Monroe consulted his cabinet. Most of his advisers told him the same thing as the former presidents, that it would be best to make the statement with the British.

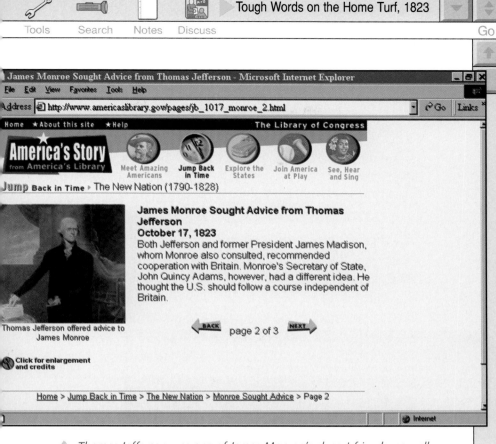

James Monroe Sought Advice from Thomas Jefferson - Microsoft Internet Explorer

File Edit View Favorites Tools Help

Address http://www.americaslibrary.gov/pages/jb_1017_monroe_2.html — Go | Links

Home ★About this site ★Help   The Library of Congress

America's Story from America's Library

Meet Amazing Americans | Jump Back in Time | Explore the States | Join America at Play | See, Hear and Sing

Jump Back in Time ▸ The New Nation (1790-1828)

James Monroe Sought Advice from Thomas Jefferson
October 17, 1823
Both Jefferson and former President James Madison, whom Monroe also consulted, recommended cooperation with Britain. Monroe's Secretary of State, John Quincy Adams, however, had a different idea. He thought the U.S. should follow a course independent of Britain.

◀BACK page 2 of 3 NEXT▶

Thomas Jefferson offered advice to James Monroe

Click for enlargement and credits

Home > Jump Back in Time > The New Nation > Monroe Sought Advice > Page 2

▲ Thomas Jefferson was one of James Monroe's closest friends, as well as a political advisor.

Although there was one dissenter. Secretary of State John Quincy Adams told Monroe that the president should state clearly and forcefully that the Western Hemisphere was off-limits. In addition, Adams, who was opinionated and hoped to be president himself someday, told Monroe that he should make the statement alone—not with the British. Adams wrote most of the message that President Monroe issued to Congress on December 2, 1823: "The American Continents are henceforth not to be considered as subjects for future colonization by any European power."[1] Those words, part of what is now

known as the Monroe Doctrine, called for an end of European colonization of the Americas. It sent a message to Russia, which had been slowly taking lands around the Pacific Coast in northwest North America, to stop. The Doctrine also promised that the United States would not interfere in the remaining European colonies in the Americas.

The message was a strongly worded statement that told all of Europe and the rest of the world—Great Britain included—to keep out of the Western Hemisphere. In a way, it was a tough statement that the United States made to the rest of the world. Whether Monroe's military could

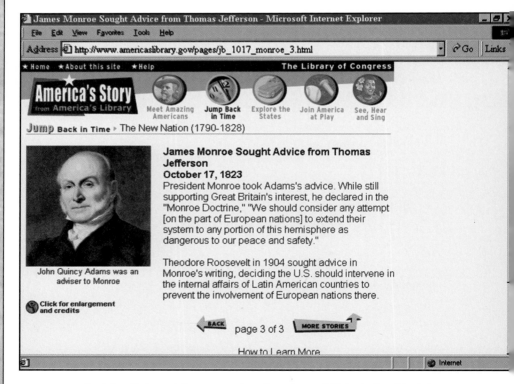

James Monroe Sought Advice from Thomas Jefferson - Microsoft Internet Explorer

File Edit View Favorites Tools Help

Address http://www.americaslibrary.gov/pages/jb_1017_monroe_3.html Go Links

★ Home   ★ About this site   ★ Help   The Library of Congress

America's Story from America's Library

Meet Amazing Americans | Jump Back in Time | Explore the States | Join America at Play | See, Hear and Sing

Jump Back in Time ▸ The New Nation (1790-1828)

James Monroe Sought Advice from Thomas Jefferson
October 17, 1823
President Monroe took Adams's advice. While still supporting Great Britain's interest, he declared in the "Monroe Doctrine," "We should consider any attempt [on the part of European nations] to extend their system to any portion of this hemisphere as dangerous to our peace and safety."

Theodore Roosevelt in 1904 sought advice in Monroe's writing, deciding the U.S. should intervene in the internal affairs of Latin American countries to prevent the involvement of European nations there.

John Quincy Adams was an adviser to Monroe

🌎 Click for enlargement and credits

◀ BACK   page 3 of 3   MORE STORIES ▶

How to Learn More

Internet

John Quincy Adams served as Secretary of State in President James Monroe's Cabinet.

actually back it up was another question. At the time, Great Britain had a much stronger navy than the United States. Had Britain decided to challenge Monroe's order, they probably would have beaten the United States in a sea battle. Yet the president and his advisers felt that they were taking a safe chance. It was unlikely that Britain would want to fight a third war against the United States.

The Americans' guess turned out to be right. No European nation tried to invade or colonize the Western Hemisphere. The president's ultimatum had worked. What Monroe likely never suspected is that nearly two hundred years later, his message would still be alive. The warning of the Monroe Doctrine still lives: Stay out of the Western Hemisphere.

Chapter 2

The Young Fighter, 1758–1775

Compared to most presidents, little is known about the childhood of James Monroe. Near the end of his life he began writing an autobiography. The book, which was never completed, included very little information about his childhood, his parents, or his schooling.

Historians do know that James's father owned land in Westmoreland County, Virginia. James was born there on April 28, 1758. His father, Spence Monroe, was a well-to-do planter and carpenter. His mother, Elizabeth, was well educated compared to other women back then. In those days, young women generally did not get an education beyond grade school. Very little has been said about Elizabeth Monroe, though her son did write that she was friendly or "amiable," and "respectable." He also called her "a good wife, and a good parent."[1] Historians do not even know exactly when she died.

▶ Young Life

As a youngster, James liked to hunt and fish. He was athletic and tall, with broad shoulders. As an adult, he grew to be six feet. James's dark hair was wavy, and he had a big nose and dimpled chin.

Even when he was very young, James developed a sense of patriotism by watching his father stand up for his beliefs. In 1766, when James was about eight years old, Spence Monroe joined other people in Virginia by criticizing the way Great Britain imposed its power on the colonies. Spence Monroe and many other Virginians

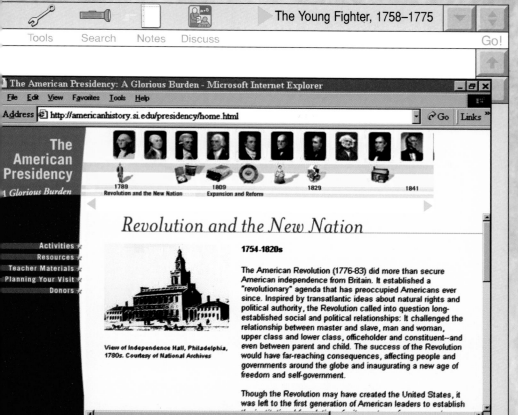

James Monroe grew up during a time of great social and political change. The American Revolution and its aftermath impacted many of his policies, especially the Monroe Doctrine.

thought Britain was being unfair, and pushed for a boycott of British goods. If colonists did not buy British products such as tea, they figured, the loss of money would send a clear message: Treat us fairly.

When he was eleven, James went to school at Campbelltown Academy. One of his classmates, John Marshall, would one day become chief justice of the United States Supreme Court. Latin and math were easier for James than most kids. He stayed at Campbelltown for five years, until age sixteen, when he experienced some major life changes. For one thing, he left Campbelltown and enrolled in a Virginia college called William & Mary. Then his father, Spence, died unexpectedly. The person now responsible for guiding James was his uncle, Joseph Jones. A member of the Continental Congress, Jones was Elizabeth Monroe's brother. Now approaching adulthood, James inherited his father's land and became responsible for taking care of his three younger brothers. He also had an older sister, but she could be responsible for herself.

▶ Joining the Revolution

The education at William & Mary, a respected school today, was not considered to be particularly good back

Engraving of Monroe - Microsoft Internet Explorer

File   Edit   View   Favorites   Tools   Help

Address http://www.swem.wm.edu/SPCOL/Monroe/monroeengraving.htm   Go   Links

Done   Internet

▲ *In 1775, the year before the Revolutionary War, Monroe dropped out of college in order to become a soldier. However, when he suffered a serious injury and could not serve in the war, he returned to school.*

▲ An artist's perception of the scene at the Battle of Trenton.

then. That was in 1774, and the colonies of America were embroiled in a deep, bitter fight with the British over taxes and political representation. Everyone knew the colonies and Great Britain were on the verge of war. James wanted to be involved, and spent most of his energy following the tensions between Great Britain and the colonies.

At William & Mary in June 1775, Monroe joined twenty-four other men in raiding the Governor's Palace arsenal, stealing 200 muskets and 300 swords that helped the revolutionary militia. One year later, as the Revolutionary War began, he dropped out of school and became a full-time soldier.

Monroe took part in the Battle of Trenton, where he injured his shoulder helping capture two cannon. After the battle he was promoted to the rank of captain. He fought in a few more battles, including the Battle of Monmouth, before returning to Virginia.

Chapter 3 ▶

Meeting Mr. Jefferson, 1780–1786

According to Thomas Jefferson, James Monroe was a good person on the inside and out. He was a friend and mentor to Monroe for forty-six years. The two met in Williamsburg, Virginia, in 1780. Jefferson, who was governor of Virginia at the time, was fifteen years older than Monroe. Even with their age difference, however, they became fast friends. Jefferson liked Monroe's intelligence and talents. Monroe admired Jefferson's ability as a leader and, like many people, was awestruck by his knack for using words. Jefferson, of course, was the lead author of the Declaration of Independence.

Since Monroe's military service had been cut short by injury, he wanted badly to find some direction in life. Jefferson had a worthy goal for his young friend. He wanted Monroe to become a lawyer. Shortly after they met, Jefferson prescribed a long list of books for Monroe to read and study.

Not long after Monroe reentered William & Mary to continue his studies, the Virginia state capital was moved from Williamsburg to Richmond. Jefferson asked Monroe to follow him there. Happy at William & Mary, Monroe was not eager to leave. Not sure what to do, he turned to his uncle, Joseph Jones, for advice. Jones advised his nephew that Jefferson was a powerful, influential man who had been kind to Monroe and could help him more in the future. "You do well to cultivate his friendship, and cannot fail to entertain a grateful sense of the favors he

Tools   Search   Notes   Discuss   Go!

WHHA - History - Microsoft Internet Explorer

File Edit View Favorites Tools Help

Address http://www.whitehousehistory.org/04_history/04_history.html   Go   Links

ELIZABETH MONROE

Romance glints from what little is known of Elizabeth Kortright's early life. She was born in New York City in 1768, to an old New York family. Because of ties to the Crown, her father had taken no active part in the War of Independence; and James Monroe wrote to his friend Thomas Jefferson that he had married the daughter of a gentleman "injured in his fortunes" by the Revolution.

Strange choice, perhaps, for a patriot veteran with political ambitions and little money of his own - but Elizabeth was beautiful, and love was decisive. They were married in February 1786, when the bride was not yet 18. His political career kept the young couple on the move as the family increased by two daughters and a son who died in infancy.

In 1794, Elizabeth accompanied her husband to France when President Washington appointed him United States minister. Arriving in the midst of the French Revolution, she took a dramatic part in saving Lafayette's wife, imprisoned and expecting death on the guillotine. The American minister's wife went to the prison and asked to see Madame Lafayette. After this hint of American interest, the prisoner was set free. Elizabeth was very popular in France, and received the affectionate name of "la belle Americaine."

For 17 years the Monroes alternated between foreign missions and service in Virginia. They made the plantation of Oak Hill their home, and appeared on the Washington scene in 1811 when James became President Madison's secretary of state.

Done   Internet

James married Elizabeth Kortright on February 16, 1786. Elizabeth played a major role in saving the life of the wife of Marquis de Lafayette, who was imprisoned and sentenced to the guillotine during the French Revolution.

has conferred upon you," Jones wrote his nephew. "I would gratify him."[1]

Meeting Mr. Madison

Following his uncle's advice, Monroe went to Richmond with the governor. He continued in his studies and, over the next couple of years, became versed in the law. Jefferson and his friends, such as future President James Madison, helped get Monroe started in politics. With guidance from Jefferson, Monroe began his political career

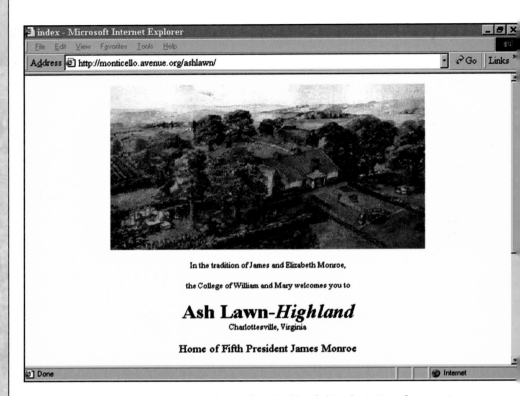

In the tradition of James and Elizabeth Monroe,

the College of William and Mary welcomes you to

Ash Lawn-*Highland*
Charlottesville, Virginia

Home of Fifth President James Monroe

▲ *Monroe and his family lived at Highland, his plantation, for twenty-four years. It is located adjacent to Jefferson's Monticello.*

when he was elected to the Virginia Assembly in 1782 at age twenty-four.

Monroe was motivated to join the Assembly because he knew he would have the chance to show off his new skills as a lawyer. Powerful leaders worked in, and watched the Assembly, and Monroe knew he could gain wealthy, influential clients by being a part of it. He then served as a member of the Congress of Confederation from 1783 to 1786, which was meeting in New York City. The Congress of Confederation had been set up by the Articles of Confederation, the document that was the blueprint for the United States' government before the Constitution.

The move to New York was a fortunate one, both politically and personally. Monroe met Elizabeth Kortright of New York, the daughter of a former British Army officer who had made a fortune as a merchant, then lost most of his money during the American Revolution. In February 1786, when Elizabeth was just seventeen, she and James married. The new Mr. and Mrs. Monroe took a short honeymoon on Long Island, then returned to New York City. They stayed there until the Congress finished its business that fall. It was then, in October 1786, that the Monroes moved back to James's home state of Virginia, beginning a journey that would eventually lead to the presidency.

Chapter 4

On the Political Rise, 1787–1816

When deciding where to live in Virginia, the Monroes picked the city of Fredericksburg. They figured that since it was a medium-sized city James Monroe could set up a law practice without competing against bigger, established firms located in Richmond. Monroe opened a law office, but was hungry to be involved in politics. First, he ran for

American Memory Digital Item Display - thc1995001877/PP - Microsoft Internet Explorer

File Edit View Favorites Tools Help

Address: oryd:@field(NUMBER+@band(thc+5a36085)):displayType=1:m856sd=thc:m856sf=5a36085 | Go | Links

Digital ID: thc 5a36085 **Source:** intermediary roll film
Retrieve uncompressed archival TIFF version (218 kilobytes)

Done | Internet

From 1786–90, Monroe operated his own law office in Fredericksburg, Virginia.

James Monroe - Microsoft Internet Explorer

File Edit View Favorites Tools Help

Address http://monticello.avenue.org/ashlawn/docs/bio-monroe.htm   Go   Links

In February 1786 James Monroe married Elizabeth Kortright of New York City. The Monroes had three children-Eliza (born December 1786), James Spence Monroe (born May 1799, died September 1800), and Maria Hester (born early 1803). For twenty-four years the Monroe family's home was HIGHLAND, Monroe's Albemarle County plantation adjacent to Jefferson's Monticello.

Monroe's fifty years of public service began with his election to the Virginia General Assembly in 1782. Subsequently, Monroe served in the Confederation Congress and in the first United States Senate; was twice Minister to France, once to Britain and to Spain; served four one-year terms as Governor of Virginia; and became President James Madison's Secretary of State and Secretary of War during the War of 1812. Monroe's greatest achievement as a diplomat was the final negotiation of the Louisiana Purchase in 1803.

Monroe's eldest daughter Eliza

Elected President of the United States in 1816 and in 1820, James Monroe resolved long-standing grievances with the British, acquired Florida from the Spanish in 1819, and proclaimed the Monroe Doctrine in 1823. Somewhat optimistically labeled the "Era of Good Feelings," Monroe's administration was hampered by the economic depression brought on by the Panic of 1819 and by the debates over the Missouri Compromise that same year. Monroe supported the American Colonization Society, which established the nation of Liberia for freed blacks. Its capital was named Monrovia in his honor. Monroe himself was torn between his belief in the "evil of slavery" and his fear of the consequences of immediate abolition.

A nationalist in diplomacy and defense, James Monroe supported a limited executive branch of the

Done   Internet

▲ Monroe's eldest daughter, Eliza.

a seat on town council, and later, he was elected to the Virginia state legislature.

A Constitutional Argument

In 1787, the same year the Monroes' first child, Eliza, was born, a group of American leaders were gathering in Philadelphia, Pennsylvania, to draft a constitution for the United States. Monroe was hoping to be invited as a delegate, but never received an invitation. Angry about this, he blamed James Madison for leaving him out. The incident caused a rift between the two men that would last for several years. Their disagreement worsened

▲ This is the first page of the Constitution of the United States. Although Monroe would have liked to join those drafting the Constitution in Philadelphia, he did not receive an invitation.

during the ratification process in Virginia, where Monroe was a member of the state convention that would vote to ratify, or approve, the Constitution. Monroe was worried that the Constitution would create a federal government that was too strong. Monroe also worried that the Constitution was flawed because it did not have a bill of rights to protect citizens' freedoms. Despite those concerns, and Monroe's vote of "no," the Constitution was ratified. The Bill of Rights was later added as the first ten Amendments.

After the Constitution was approved by the states, Monroe ran for one of Virginia's seats in the House of Representatives. He lost that race to Madison, but was elected to the United States Senate in 1790. As a senator, Monroe joined a group of anti-Federalist politicians led by Jefferson. That group favored limiting the power of the federal government, and putting much of the power in the hands of the individual states. The Federalists, on the other hand, wanted to expand the powers of the federal government.

At the time, Great Britain and France dominated the world with their militaries. France was in the midst of its own revolution to topple the king and bring in a more democratic form of government. Jefferson and Monroe's group of politicians, who formed a party known as the Democrat-Republicans, supported the idea of France becoming a republic with elected officials instead of a monarchy ruled by a king. The Federalists, meanwhile, usually supported policies that favored a strong alliance with Great Britain.

▶ A Life in France

President George Washington felt that the United States should remain neutral, or not take sides, in the French Revolution, which lasted from 1789 to 1799. Monroe agreed with President Washington's policy of neutrality, though he was sympathetic to the French cause. Because of that, President Washington appointed Monroe as minister to France in 1794. By doing that, the president hoped that he would ease the fears of French people who believed that the United States was favoring Britain.

Monroe blended well into French life. He and Elizabeth made many friends and fell in love with the

▲ *Marquis de Lafayette.*

elegant culture of France. Two years after he arrived, Monroe knew the language so well that he no longer needed an interpreter. But he never forgot his revolutionary beginnings. One day, he was walking in Paris with his daughter, Eliza, who was studying at a French school. Monroe told his daughter that the United States was really a better country than France, even though it was much younger and did not have the fine castles and cathedrals of the older European nations. "Yes, papa," Eliza answered. "But we haven't any roads like this." "That's true," Monroe replied. "Our country may be likened to a new house. We lack many things, but we possess the most precious of all—liberty!"[1]

The mission in France was to represent the United States, but the Monroes stretched their political duties far beyond. For example, when the wife of Revolutionary War hero Marquis de Lafayette was about to be executed on the guillotine, Elizabeth Monroe spoke on her behalf and saved her life.

While the Monroes enjoyed their time in Europe, not

◀ *Elizabeth Monroe.*

everyone was happy with him back home. The Federalists, led by George Washington and Alexander Hamilton, thought Monroe was not neutral enough. In particular, one speech he made to the French Assembly praising the Republic of France angered President Washington. In September 1796, Washington recalled Monroe, ending his diplomatic mission.

"If Mr. Monroe should ever fill the Chair of Government, he may . . . let the French Minister frame his speeches," Washington said. "There is abundant evidence of his being a mere tool in the hands of the French government."[2]

▶ Back Home

Once back in Virginia in June 1797, Monroe was so bitter about his firing that he refused to visit his former commander, President Washington, at Mount Vernon. In a letter, Monroe even called the first president "insane." He also wrote a document defending his actions in France. How strongly did Monroe feel? The paper he wrote was 407 pages long.[3]

When President Washington ▶ ended Monroe's diplomatic mission in France, Monroe wrote him an angry letter.

Many people thought that Monroe's career as a politician was over. What happened was exactly the opposite. Many of the Democrat-Republicans were impressed by his brash self-confidence and strong beliefs. Now more closely allied than ever with Jefferson's party, Monroe was elected governor of Virginia for consecutive one-year terms from 1799 to 1803.

Although things were generally quiet in Virginia during this time, the national and international news was far from silent. Thomas Jefferson, the president of the United States at that time, appointed Monroe on a mission to France. The diplomatic team was to negotiate with Napoléon, the French leader, to buy the huge area of North American land known as Louisiana. In 1803, the Louisiana Purchase doubled the size of the country. In addition, while James and Elizabeth were in France, their second daughter, Maria, was born in Paris.

Almost as soon as the Louisiana negotiations were done, Monroe went to England. The British Navy had been harassing U.S. ships bound for France. Monroe's mission was to talk the British into leaving American ships alone. That mission, however, did not work. Next, Monroe was sent to Spain to try and negotiate a treaty to sell part of Florida.

Although Madison and Monroe were once close friends, Madison's run for president caused a rift in their relationship.

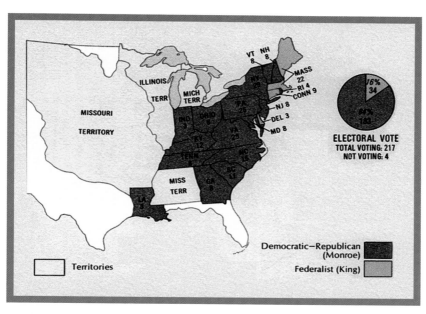

VT 8 NH 8
MASS 22
NY 29
RI 4
CONN 9
NJ 8
PA 25
DEL 3
MD 8
IND 3
OHIO 8
VA 25
KY 12
TENN 8
NC 15
SC 11
GA 8
ILLINOIS
MICH TERR
MISSOURI TERRITORY
MISS TERR
LA 3

76%
34

84%
183

ELECTORAL VOTE
TOTAL VOTING: 217
NOT VOTING: 4

Democratic–Republican (Monroe)
Federalist (King)

Territories

This map shows the results of the presidential election of 1816.

That, too, proved fruitless, and Monroe eventually returned to the United States late in 1807.

Upon his return, one faction of the Democratic-Republican Party wanted him to run for president in 1808. That offer strained Monroe's relationship with James Madison even more. Jefferson was stepping down as president, and had chosen Madison to run as his successor. With Jefferson's support behind Madison, Monroe agreed to step aside and not run. He was not happy, though, and Monroe's relationship with both Jefferson and Madison (who did win the election) was frosty for the next few years.[4]

Friends Again

Their friendship was rekindled in 1811, when President Madison asked Monroe to be his secretary of state.

Monroe took the job at a critical time. Diplomatic relations with Great Britain strained and finally broke with the War of 1812. In 1814, shortly after the British burned Washington, D.C., Madison also appointed Monroe secretary of war. He kept that job until the battles ended in 1815.

At the end of Madison's second term, Monroe was Democratic-Republicans' natural choice to run for president. He was accomplished and qualified and, what is more, had the support of President Madison. Daniel D. Tompkins, the governor of New York, was chosen to run for vice president. The opposing Federalist Party had been losing popularity with voters, particularly because it had not supported the War of 1812.

In the 1816 campaign for the presidency, Monroe faced Federalist Rufus King and won easily, taking every state except Massachusetts, Connecticut, and Delaware. Thirty-six years after Thomas Jefferson had kindled his interest in the law and politics, James Monroe had now reached the most powerful, important platform in the country. He was the fifth president of the United States.

Chapter 5

Problem Solver, 1817–1824

James Monroe took the oath of office in January 1817, but he had no place to live. During the War of 1812, the British had attacked Washington, D.C., and burnt the executive mansion. The president's home was scorched so badly that it would take years to rebuild. When the building was finished, it was covered with a coat of white paint, and was thus renamed the White House. The refurbished mansion was not ready for the first family when he was inaugurated in 1817, so Monroe decided to begin his presidency by traveling the country.

For the next fifteen weeks, Monroe visited cities across the nation, traveling north from Washington to Maine, then west to Michigan, and finally trekking southeast back to the capital. In almost every place he visited, Monroe was greeted by cheering crowds. Even the citizens of New England, an area known for supporting the Federalists, cheered the president. Watching New Englanders support an opposition party president, a writer from the *Boston Columbian Centinel* newspaper called this the "era of good feelings."[1] It was a label that would stick. Even today, historians remember Monroe's presidency (1817–25) as the Era of Good Feelings.

This was a time when Monroe's Democratic-Republican Party was strong. Other political parties—such as the Federalist Party—were divided and weak. Monroe wished that political parties did not even exist. "Surely our government may prosper without the existence of parties," he said. "I have always considered their existence as the curse of the country, of which we have sufficient proof, more especially in the late war."[2]

▶ The End of A Different Kind of Party

During the next eight years, Monroe's administration would be a political success. However, a big part of White House tradition is the social functions that take place there. The president and, especially, the first lady are expected to entertain high-powered guests and hold extravagant parties. At this, the Monroes failed.

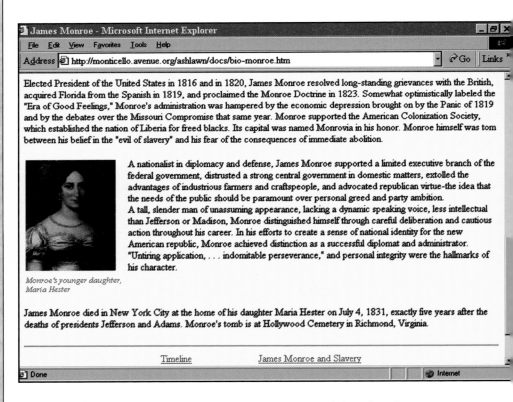

James Monroe - Microsoft Internet Explorer

File   Edit   View   Favorites   Tools   Help

Address http://monticello.avenue.org/ashlawn/docs/bio-monroe.htm   Go   Links

Elected President of the United States in 1816 and in 1820, James Monroe resolved long-standing grievances with the British, acquired Florida from the Spanish in 1819, and proclaimed the Monroe Doctrine in 1823. Somewhat optimistically labeled the "Era of Good Feelings," Monroe's administration was hampered by the economic depression brought on by the Panic of 1819 and by the debates over the Missouri Compromise that same year. Monroe supported the American Colonization Society, which established the nation of Liberia for freed blacks. Its capital was named Monrovia in his honor. Monroe himself was torn between his belief in the "evil of slavery" and his fear of the consequences of immediate abolition.

A nationalist in diplomacy and defense, James Monroe supported a limited executive branch of the federal government, distrusted a strong central government in domestic matters, extolled the advantages of industrious farmers and craftspeople, and advocated republican virtue-the idea that the needs of the public should be paramount over personal greed and party ambition.

A tall, slender man of unassuming appearance, lacking a dynamic speaking voice, less intellectual than Jefferson or Madison, Monroe distinguished himself through careful deliberation and cautious action throughout his career. In his efforts to create a sense of national identity for the new American republic, Monroe achieved distinction as a successful diplomat and administrator. "Untiring application, . . . indomitable perseverance," and personal integrity were the hallmarks of his character.

Monroe's younger daughter, Maria Hester

James Monroe died in New York City at the home of his daughter Maria Hester on July 4, 1831, exactly five years after the deaths of presidents Jefferson and Adams. Monroe's tomb is at Hollywood Cemetery in Richmond, Virginia.

Timeline   James Monroe and Slavery

Done   Internet

▲ Monroe's youngest daughter, Maria, and her fiancé, Samuel Gouverneur, were the first couple ever married in the White House.

Part of the fault rested with Mrs. Monroe, and part with former First Lady Dolley Madison. Few could compare to the outgoing and popular Mrs. Madison, so Mrs. Monroe struggled from the start. For one thing, she was often sick and had to cut back on her official duties. For another thing, she ended the practice of paying courtesy calls on other members of the Washington elite, such as the wives of senators and Cabinet members. And even though the White House was often open for weekly parties, the Monroes decided to keep the guest list small for the wedding of their daughter, Maria Hester Monroe. The wedding of Maria and Samuel Gouverneur was the first wedding performed in the White House, and many people thought it should have been a lavish party, not the small ceremony that it was.

The South and the West

Of course, Monroe faced bigger problems while in office. The Panic of 1819 was a two-year financial crisis that hit the western territories especially hard. Among the causes were that the Bank of the United States was lending too much money, and there was more competition from European imports. In response, the government made it easier for people to get loans for buying land. That made it simpler to purchase land out west, and it got people spending money again.

There was also the fight in Congress over the Missouri Compromise of 1820, which admitted Missouri to the Union as a slave state and Maine as a free state. It was also decided that land north of the 35°30′ latitude line in the Louisiana Purchase territory would be slave-free. Land south of the line would be slave-holding states. The fighting to work out a compromise was bitter and it divided

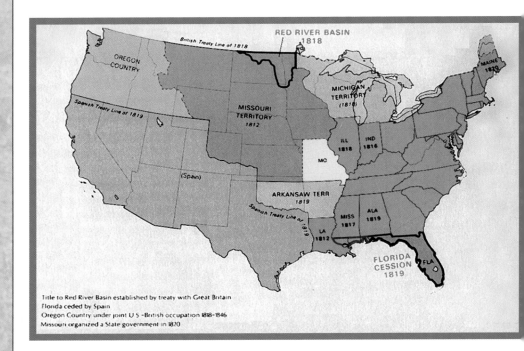

Title to Red River Basin established by treaty with Great Britain
Florida ceded by Spain
Oregon Country under joint U S -British occupation 1818-1846
Missouri organized a State government in 1820

▲ This map shows the territorial growth of the United States in 1820.

people between the North and South. Seeing the danger of such anger, former President Jefferson in 1820 warned everyone that the issue of slavery was "like a firebell in the night"[3] for the young country. His words proved to be true when the Civil War started in 1861.

Henry Clay, who was Speaker of the House and had been a key person in developing the Missouri Compromise, introduced his American System to Congress in 1822. The system called for canals and roads to be built at federal expense. President Monroe's only presidential veto squashed federal funds for the National Road. Keeping with his belief that a smaller federal government was better, he believed the states should pay for roads and canals.

Foreign Friends and Foes

Thanks mainly to Secretary of State John Quincy Adams, whom historians credit as being one of the best in history, President Monroe was usually successful in dealing with other countries. For example, the president dispatched General Andrew Jackson to the border of Spanish Florida in 1817. His job was to stop the Seminole Indians and escaped slaves from going on raids into Georgia.

Jackson went beyond his orders and, in 1818, invaded Florida. That incident convinced the Spanish that they could not hold Florida, so they decided to give it up. In 1819, Secretary of State Adams negotiated a treaty with Spanish Minister Luis de Oñis in which Spain sold Florida to the United States.

Adams was also able to negotiate the Convention of 1818, which settled the U.S.-Canadian border at the 49th parallel from Minnesota to the Rocky Mountains. It also set aside American and British claims to Oregon with the agreement that both nations could settle the region for ten years.

A Doctrine for History

The treaties with Spain and Britain allowed the United States to continue expanding its size across North America. Still, the achievement that President Monroe and Secretary Adams will be remembered for best is the Monroe Doctrine, which was first issued as a message to Congress in 1823. In response to European threats to retake Spain's lost American colonies, Adams wrote a message that President Monroe sent to Congress on December 2, 1823. The document called for an end of colonization by Europe in the Americas and pledged that the United

▲ *Henry Clay, Speaker of the House of Representatives.*

States would not interfere in the remaining European colonies in the hemisphere.

In 1823, Adams, with Monroe's approval, wrote to the American minister in St. Petersburg to tell the Russians that it was time to quit trying to set up trading posts and settlements in northwestern North America. His message was simple: "The future peace of the world and the interest of Russia herself cannot be promoted by Russian settlements upon any part of the American Continent," Adams wrote. "With the exception of the British establishments north of the United States, the remainder of the American continents must henceforth be left to the management of American hands."[4]

▶ Not All "Good Feelings"

America's feelings were not good all the time. Political bickering still echoed in Congress. In Monroe's own Democratic-Republican Party, politicians who wanted to succeed him as president had their own arguments. For example, one man who aspired to be president was Secretary of the Treasury William Crawford. Knowing that it would help his chances if he had friends working in important jobs, Secretary Crawford gave a list of their names to Monroe. The president delayed acting on the matter. So one day, Secretary Crawford stormed into the president's office and demanded to know why his friends had not been put in office. President Monroe said he would not appoint any of them, which angered Secretary Crawford so much that he lunged at the president with his cane. The president grabbed a pair of tongs from a fireplace to defend himself and ordered Secretary Crawford out of the White House.[5]

▶ Leaving Office

From the Panic of 1819, to the threat of Europe invading the Western Hemisphere, James Monroe faced many problems. He solved them, too. Not every solution was the best. The Missouri Compromise, for instance, delayed the Civil War for forty-one years, but it did not solve the slavery problem or prevent the war. The Monroe administration did keep the country running smoothly and quieted most of the president's critics. In fact, Monroe was so well-liked that he did not even face an opponent when he ran for reelection in 1820.

That "Era of Good Feelings" could not last forever. At the

William Crawford. ▶

end of Monroe's second term, he was ready to retire. As the president left, so did political harmony. Four candidates ran for the White House in 1824, but none won a majority of votes in the electoral college. Congress had to decide the outcome, and John Quincy Adams eventually won. Monroe stayed out of the election because, in his words, he found it "improper, on principle, to take any part in the election, or even to be suspected of doing it. I keep myself as abstracted from it as I possibly can."[6]

Last of the Virginians, 1825–1831

Tired of dealing with personal insults and attacks—especially the one by Secretary William Crawford—Monroe was ready to leave Washington by the end of his second term. "I shall be happy," he wrote, "when I can retire beyond their reach in peace to my farm."[1]

Monroe did that in March 1825. James and Elizabeth retired to their Virginia estate, called Oak Hill, which had been designed by Thomas Jefferson. After so many years of government service, Monroe was about $75,000 in debt. Blaming this on the low salaries he earned while serving in political office (Monroe's presidential salary was $25,000 per year), he believed the government should help him pay off the debts. Eventually, Monroe was able to convince Congress to cover part of the amount. He received approximately $30,000.

During the next five years, Monroe continued to serve in public positions. He was a member of the board of regents for the University of Virginia and participated in the Virginia Constitutional Convention. At the same time, however, he was intent on protecting his privacy. To make sure nobody could easily examine his life in detail, Monroe destroyed all of his personal papers.

After Elizabeth Monroe died in 1830, James moved from Oak Hill to New York City to live with his daughter, Maria, and her husband, Samuel Gouverneur. Monroe spent time writing two books—one about his life, the other about the American government.

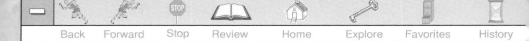
Unfortunately for historians, neither book was ever finished. Not long after his move to New York, Monroe became sick. His illness started with a bad cough and grew worse. Monroe died of heart failure on July 4, 1831. He was buried in New York City three days later. In 1858, Monroe's body was moved to Virginia, where it remains today.

▶ The Virginian's Legacy

James Monroe was one of America's first professional politicians. Today, some people are wary of those who

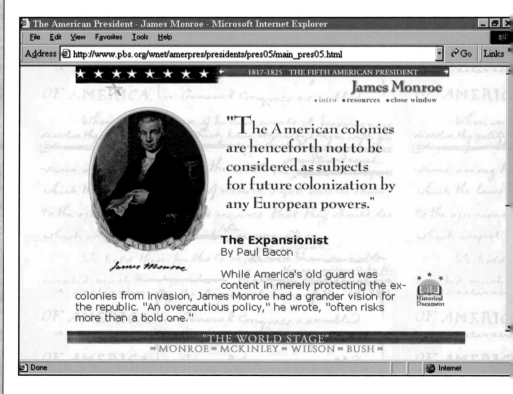

The American President - James Monroe - Microsoft Internet Explorer

File   Edit   View   Favorites   Tools   Help

Address http://www.pbs.org/wnet/amerpres/presidents/pres05/main_pres05.html   Go   Links

★ ★ ★ ★ ★ ★ ★ ★ ★   1817-1825   THE FIFTH AMERICAN PRESIDENT

James Monroe
•intro •resources •close window

"The American colonies are henceforth not to be considered as subjects for future colonization by any European powers."

The Expansionist
By Paul Bacon

While America's old guard was content in merely protecting the ex-colonies from invasion, James Monroe had a grander vision for the republic. "An overcautious policy," he wrote, "often risks more than a bold one."

Historical Document

"THE WORLD STAGE"
MONROE ∞ MCKINLEY ∞ WILSON ∞ BUSH

Done   Internet

▲ James Monroe is perhaps most remembered for the Monroe Doctrine, which bears his name.

spend most of their adult lives serving in political office. But Monroe had a clean reputation. Even one of the most influential men in America, Thomas Jefferson, said so. Talking to his friend, James Madison, Jefferson once said, "Turn his soul wrongside outwards, and there is not a speck on it."[2]

One of America's first professional politicians, James Monroe proved that a person could make a career out of public service. The path he took to the White House— becoming a lawyer, then rising through the levels of local, state, and national politics—has been followed by count-less politicians ever since. Monroe is remembered as a president who was able to overcome challenges. He pushed the country through the financial panic of 1819. His Missouri Compromise prevented war—for a while, at least. Through the Monroe Doctrine, he told the world that the United States considered both North and South America as its sphere of influence. That policy helped to keep the Western Hemisphere free of colonial invasion for nearly two centuries.

Unlike some presidents, Monroe's solutions were not glorious or dramatic. For example, Abraham Lincoln's Emancipation Proclamation has become a famous part of American History. Still, Monroe's policies worked well enough to create the Era of Good Feelings. Never has the United States been so politically peaceful as it was during the years of the Monroe presidency. Secretary of the State John Quincy Adams once said that he felt that Monroe's terms in office may be considered the "golden age" of the republic.[3]

Monroe is not the most famous of the early presidents, but his place in history is secure next to George Washington, Thomas Jefferson, and James Madison.

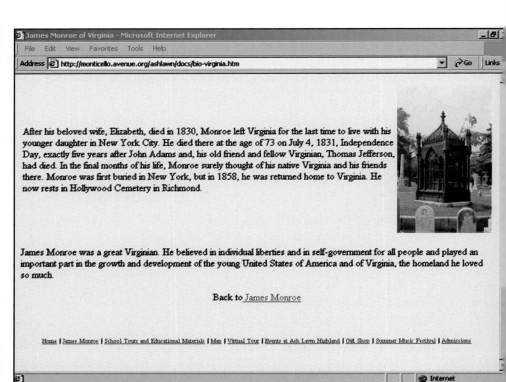

▲ *James Monroe's grave in Virginia.*

Those four men are remembered as the "Virginia Dynasty." Each of them was from Virginia and became one of the first five presidents of the United States. Monroe was the last of the Virginia Dynasty, but like Washington, Jefferson, and Madison, his work and words still live today.

Chapter Notes

Chapter 1. Tough Words on the Home Turf, 1823

1. John Sutherland Bonnell, *Presidential Profiles* (Philadelphia: The Westminster Press, 1971), pp. 45–46.

Chapter 2. The Young Fighter, 1758–1775

1. William A. DeGregorio, *The Complete Book of U.S. Presidents* (New York: Dembner Books, 1984), p. 74.

Chapter 3. Meeting Mr. Jefferson, 1780–1786

1. Harry Ammon, *James Monroe: The Quest for National Identity* (Charlottesville: University Press of Virginia, 1990), p. 31.

Chapter 4. On the Political Rise, 1787–1816

1. Paul F. Boller, Jr., *Presidential Anecdotes* (New York: Oxford University Press, 1981), p. 53.

2. William A. DeGregorio, *The Complete Book of U.S. Presidents* (New York: Dembner Books, 1984), pp. 84–85.

3. Philip B. Kunhardt, Jr., Philip B. Kunhardt III, and Peter W. Kunhardt, *The American President* (New York: Riverhead Books/Penguin Putnam, 1999), pp. 307–308.

4. James Madison Center at James Madison University, "Brief Biography: James Madison, Madison in Power," *James Madison University Home Page,* 1999, <www.jmu.edu/madison/biography/power.htm> (February 22, 2002).

Chapter 5. Problem Solver, 1817–1824

1. Noble E. Cunningham, Jr., *The Presidency of James Monroe* (Lawrence: The University Press of Kansas, 1996), pp. 37–38.

2. William A. DeGregorio, *The Complete Book of U.S. Presidents* (New York: Dembner Books, 1984), p. 85.

3. Paul F. Boller Jr., *Presidential Anecdotes* (New York: Penguin Books, 1981), pp. 52–53.

4. Cunningham, p. 152.

5. Boller, p. 52.

6. Cunningham, p. 179.

Chapter 6. Last of the Virginians, 1825–1831

1. Philip B. Kunhardt, Jr., Philip B. Kunhardt III, and Peter W. Kunhardt, *The American President* (New York: Riverhead Books/Penguin Putnam, 1999), p. 309.

2. William A. DeGregorio, *The Complete Book of U.S. Presidents* (New York: Dembner Books, 1984), p. 84.

3. Charles Francis Adams, ed., *Memoirs of John Quincy Adams*, vol. 6 (Philadelphia, 1874–77), as quoted in Paul F. Boller, Jr., *Presidential Anecdotes* (New York: Oxford Press, 1981), p. 53.

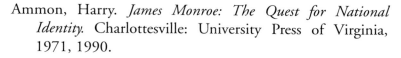

Further Reading

Ammon, Harry. *James Monroe: The Quest for National Identity.* Charlottesville: University Press of Virginia, 1971, 1990.

Boller, Jr., Paul F. *Presidential Anecdotes.* New York: Oxford University Press, 1996.

Garrison, Webb. *A Treasury of White House Tales.* Nashville, Tenn.: Rutledge Hill Press, 1996.

Green, Carl R. *The Revolutionary War.* Berkeley Heights, N.J.: MyReportLinks.com Books, 2002.

Kelley, Brent P. *James Monroe.* Broomall, Pa.: Chelsea House, 2000.

Krull, Kathleen. *Lives of the Presidents.* San Diego, Calif.: Harcourt Brace, 1998.

Kunhardt, Jr., Philip B. et. al. *The American President.* New York: Penguin Putnam, 1999.

Old, Wendie C. *James Monroe.* Springfield, N.J.: Enslow Publishers, Inc., 1997.

Stefoff, Rebecca. *James Monroe: 5th President of the United States.* Ada, Okla.: Garrett Educational Corporation, 1988.

Welsbacher, Anne. *James Monroe.* Minneapolis, Minn.: ABDO Publishing Company, 1998.

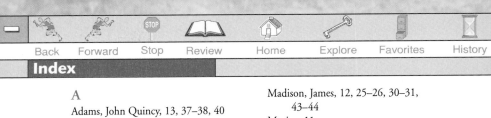